A Mother's Nature

A Mother's Nature

Quips, Quotes and Musings on Motherhood

BY MELISSA SOVEY

WILLOW CREEK PRESS®

Published by Willow Creek Press, Inc.
P.O. Box 147, Minocqua, Wisconsin 54548

Photo Credits: p2 © Photoshot/Masterfile; p5 © Theo Allofs/Masterfile; p7 © Masterfile;
p8 © Minden Pictures/Masterfile; p11 © Minden Pictures/Masterfile;
p12 © Jeremy Woodhouse/Masterfile; p15 © Minden Pictures/Masterfile;
p16 © Minden Pictures/Masterfile; p19 © Minden Pictures/Masterfile;
p20 © Minden Pictures/Masterfile; p23 © Minden Pictures/Masterfile;
p24 © F. Lukasseck/Masterfile; p27 © Minden Pictures/Masterfile;
p28 © Londolozi/Masterfile; p31 © Minden Pictures/Masterfile;
p32 © Minden Pictures/Masterfile; p35 © Minden Pictures/Masterfile;
p36 © F. Lukasseck/Masterfile; p39 © Minden Pictures/Masterfile;
p40 © Minden Pictures/Masterfile; p43 © Minden Pictures/Masterfile;
p44 © Minden Pictures/Masterfile; p47 © Frank Krahmer/Masterfile;
p48 © Ken & Michelle Dyball/Masterfile; p51 © Minden Pictures/Masterfile;
p52 © Minden Pictures/Masterfile; p55 © Theo Allofs/Masterfile;
p56 © Minden Pictures/Masterfile; p59 © Minden Pictures/Masterfile;
p60 © Minden Pictures/Masterfile; p63 © Minden Pictures/Masterfile;
p64 © Minden Pictures/Masterfile; p67 © Photoshot/Masterfile; p68 © Minden Pictures/Masterfile;
p71 © Minden Pictures/Masterfile; p72 © Minden Pictures/Masterfile;
p75 © F. Lukasseek/Masterfile; p76 © Minden Pictures/Masterfile;
p79 © Minden Pictures/Masterfile; p80 © Jamie Scarrow/Masterfile;
p83 © Minden Pictures/Masterfile; p84 © Photoshot/Masterfile;
p87 © Gloria H. Chomica/Masterfile; p88 © Chris Hendrickson/Masterfile;
p91 © Londolozi/Masterfile; p92 © Ken & Michelle Dyball/Masterfile;
p95 © Photoshot/Masterfile; p96 © Ken & Michelle Dyball/Masterfile

Design: Donnie Rubo
Printed in Canada

"In the beginning there was my mother. A shape.
A shape and a force, standing in the light. You
could see her energy; it was visible in the air.
Against any background she stood out."

—Marilyn Krysl

However a child arrives in a woman's life, she can't help but be awestruck by the mystery of life in all its delicacies and strengths.

"Miracles, in the sense of phenomena we cannot explain, surround us on every hand: life itself is the miracle of miracles."

—George Bernard Shaw

"I just can't get over how much babies cry. I really had
no idea what I was getting into. To tell you the truth,
I thought it would be more like getting a cat."

—Anne Lamott

Becoming a mother is an eye-opening experience. In fact, there will be more eye-openers than shut-eye.

With motherhood comes a new sense of adaptability. The word "schedule" takes on a whole new meaning.

"Home alone with a wakeful newborn,
I could shower so quickly that the mirror
didn't fog and the backs of my knees stayed dry."
—Marni Jackson

"In the evening, after she has gone to sleep,
I kneel beside the crib and touch her face,
where it is pressed against the slats, with mine."

—Joan Didion

A mother may long for bedtime, but still watch her sleeping child for hours.

And then there is the miracle of
just how profoundly and intensely
motherhood redefines love.

"In the sheltered simplicity of the first days
after a baby is born, one sees again the
magical closed circle, the miraculous sense
of two people existing only for each other."

—Anne Morrow Lindbergh

"The real religion of the world comes from women
much more than from men — from mothers most of all,
who carry the key of our souls in their bosoms."

—Oliver Wendell Holmes

Life takes on an entirely new meaning and importance.

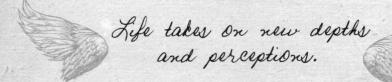

Life takes on new depths and perceptions.

"Becoming a mother makes you the mother of all children. From now on each wounded, abandoned, frightened child is yours. You live in the suffering mothers of every race and creed and weep with them. You long to comfort all who are desolate."

—Charlotte Gray

And along with new views of the world, self-perception changes as well.

"Motherhood brings as much joy as ever, but it still brings boredom, exhaustion, and sorrow too. Nothing else ever will make you as happy or as sad, as proud or as tired, for nothing is quite as hard as helping a person develop his own individuality especially while you struggle to keep your own."

—Marguerite Kelly and Elia Parsons

Sometimes moms don't even feel like their bodies are their own anymore.

"Over the years I have learned that motherhood
is much like an austere religious order, the
joining of which obligates one to relinquish
all claims to personal possessions."

—Nancy Stahl

"A mother's love for her child is like nothing else in the world. It knows no law, no pity, it dares all things and crushes down remorselessly all that stands in its path"

—Agatha Christie

Mothers soon discover a primal
strength they never knew they had.

Motherhood often requires tremendous sacrifices, and it certainly carries with it immense responsibility.

"Everybody knows that a good mother gives her children a feeling of trust and stability. She is their earth. She is the one they can count on for the things that matter most of all. She is their food and their bed and the extra blanket when it grows cold in the night; she is their warmth and their health and their shelter; she is the one they want to be near when they cry."

—Katharine Butler Hathaway

"It's the three pairs of eyes that mothers have to have...
one pair that sees through closed doors. Another in the back
of her head... and, of course, the ones in front that can
look at a child when he goofs up and reflect 'I understand
and I love you' without so much as uttering a word."

—Erma Bombeck

Motherhood requires growing up...
however there will be many reminders
of our own childhood antics and,
consequently, reminders of our
own mother's wisdom.

Along the way, moms learn
to take good advice, to trust
their instincts, and to take
time to just relax and enjoy.

"Parents are often so busy with the physical rearing of
children that they miss the glory of parenthood, just as
the grandeur of the trees is lost when raking leaves."

—Marcelene Cox

"A child can always teach an adult three things:
to be happy for no reason, to always be busy
with something, and to know how to demand
with all his might that which he desires."

—Paulo Coelho

Motherhood requires resolve, consistency and persistence.

Along with unlimited patience,
motherhood requires a sense of humor.

"My children... have been a constant
joy to me (except on the days they weren't)."

—Evelyn Fairbanks

"Before becoming a mother I had a hundred theories on how to bring up children. Now I have seven children and only one theory: love them, especially when they least deserve to be loved."

—Kate Samperi

Most of mothering is just figuring things out as you go along.

Love is the basic ingredient of mothering. It drives every decision. It is unconditional.

"Mother's love is peace.
It need not be acquired,
it need not be deserved."

—Erich Fromm

Mothering is a constant state of awareness combined with the uncanny ability to sense danger where danger never seemed to lurk before.

"The story of a mother's life:
Trapped between a scream and a hug."
—Cathy Guisewite

No one knows better than a mother
how many different directions a person
can be stretched at one time or what
it really means to multi-task.

"Mother had a thousand thoughts to get through within
a day, and most of these were about avoiding disaster."

—Natalie Kusz

"Family faces are magic mirrors. Looking at people who belong to us, we see the past, present and future. We make discoveries about ourselves."

—Gail Lumet Buckley

Motherhood can also
be quiet, reflective, and
incredibly revealing.

Matricaria
Chamomilla

A mother is an attentive listener,
knowing that she is often the
first sounding-board.

"It was my mother who gave me my voice. She did this, I know now, by clearing a space where my words could fall, grow, then find their way to others."

—Paula Giddings

"If a child lives with approval, he learns to live with himself."

—Dorothy Law Nolte

A mother's time, attention, and patient reassurances can never be underestimated.

Motherhood is full of surprises.
Many, many surprises.

"A mother is neither cocky, nor proud, because she knows the school principal may call at any minute to report that her child had just driven a motorcycle through the gymnasium."

—Mary Kay Blakely

"I cannot forget my mother. She is my bridge.
When I needed to get across, she steadied
herself long enough for me to run across safely."

—Renita Weems

When the courage of a child
wanes, a mother carries on, though
she might have fears of her own.
Two leaders are born.

Motherhood is a fortress of solace,
a haven, and a refuge of comfort
where words are not necessary
because the heart speaks.

"I want to lean into her the way
wheat leans into the wind."

—Louise Erdrich

Motherhood is playful and spirited, silly and joyful.

"My mom is a neverending song in my heart of comfort, happiness, and being. I may sometimes forget the words but I always remember the tune."

—Graycie Harmon

It is often said that there
is no such thing as a
non-working mother.

"I looked on child rearing not only as a work of love and
duty but as a profession that was fully as interesting
and challenging as any honorable profession in the world
and one that demanded the best that I could bring to it."

—Rose Kennedy

"Parents teach in the toughest school in the world: The School for Making People. You are the board of education, the principal, the classroom teacher, and the janitor."

—Virginia Satir

Each mother is preparing her child to be the best member of society he or she can be.

And each mother is forming
a family role model.

"Our children are not going to be just "our children" —
they are going to be other people's husbands and wives
and the parents of our grandchildren."

—Mary S. Calderone

Being a mother means being introduced to something new every day.

"If a child is to keep alive his inborn sense of wonder, he needs the companionship of at least one adult who can share it, rediscovering with him the joy, excitement and mystery of the world we live in."

—Rachel Carson

Motherhood means learning more about life than you could have imagined, and from the most unlikely sources.

"Parents learn a lot from their
children about coping with life."
—Muriel Spark

"Some mothers are kissing mothers and some are scolding mothers, but it is love just the same, and most mothers kiss and scold together."

—Pearl S. Buck

Motherhood is tough, exhausting and often includes episodes that would try the patience of a saint.

There are no perfect mothers. There will be times in motherhood where humble apologies need to be offered.

"Yes, Mother. I can see you are flawed. You have not hidden it. That is your greatest gift to me."

—Alice Walker

"If you want children to keep their feet on the ground, put some responsibility on their shoulders."

—Abigail Van Buren

There are so many "firsts"
that are both wonderful and
scary at the same time.

There are so many times when a
mother wants to run to the rescue
when she knows she should not.

"The finest inheritance you can give to a
child is to allow it to make its own way,
completely on its own feet."

—Isadora Duncan

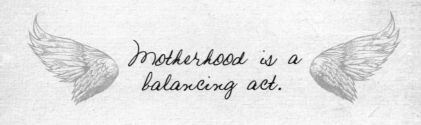

Motherhood is a balancing act.

"Instant availability without continuous presence
is probably the best role a mother can play."

—Lotte Bailyn

Mothering means knowing how to pick and choose your battles.

"Mothers are basically a patient lot.
They have to be or they would devour their
offspring early on, like guppies."

—Mary Daheim

"Mother — that was the bank where we deposited all our hurts and worries."

—T. DeWitt Talmage

Mothering means knowing when
troubles aren't so small anymore,
setting examples and helping
to find solutions.

Motherhood also means being vulnerable to all the trials and tribulations of raising a child, and the inherent risk of heartache.

"Life is not meant to be easy, my child;
but take courage: it can be delightful."

—George Bernard Shaw

Although some days don't feel like it, childhood seems to fly by. Each stage brings new rewards and challenges and growing pains to deal with for mother and child alike.

"Mother Nature is providential. She gives us twelve years to develop a love for our children before turning them into teenagers."
—William Galvin

After all, the purpose
of parenting is to give
wings to our offspring.

"Adolescence is perhaps nature's way of
preparing parents to welcome the empty nest."

—Karen Savage and Patricia Adams

"When I stopped seeing my mother with the eyes of a child,
I saw the woman who helped me give birth to myself."

—Nancy Friday

The payoff is worth all of the effort.

The rewards are many and are lifelong.

"I love my mother as the trees love water and sunshine —
she helps me grow, prosper, and reach great heights."

—Adabella Radici

"The tie which links mother and child is of such pure and immaculate strength as to be never violated."
—Washington Irving

No matter the distance,
no matter the age, there are
no boundaries to mother-love.

The memories are sweet and the mother-child bond is eternal.

"A mother's happiness is like a beacon, lighting up the future but reflected also on the past in the guise of fond memories."

—Honore' de Balzac

"Motherhood: All love
begins and ends there."
—Robert Browning